THE SOUL IN YOURSELF

— Unlocking Your Inner Resilience

Rediscovering the Inner Power within oneself

By Mahua Sil Sett, Master of Economics, LL.B.

मा
mahuasilsettbooks

Published in India.

For permissions, contact: Email: mahuasilsettbooks@gmail.com

ISBN: 978-93-343-8903-6 (Paperback)

ISBN 978-93-343-8903-6

9 789334 389036

Preface

In today's fast-moving and demanding world, many people feel tired, not just in body but in spirit. There is noise everywhere, from outside pressures to the silent storms within. We try to keep up and stay strong, but we often forget that true strength does not come from pushing through at all costs. It comes from listening, reflecting, and returning to ourselves.

This book was written to guide you back to that quiet, strong part of yourself. The part that speaks in moments of stillness, that helps you rise even after falling, that knows your worth is not measured by success but by soulfulness. ***The Soul In Yourself*** is not meant to give quick solutions or preach perfect answers. Instead, it gently invites you to look inward and discover your own resilience, the kind that grows through time, tenderness, and understanding.

Many of us go through life carrying silent weight, such as worries we do not speak of, feelings we barely understand, and moments that shake our inner balance. We keep going, trying to be strong and trying to meet expectations. But deep down, we often forget who we truly are. We forget that strength is not loud or harsh. Sometimes, strength is gentle. Sometimes, it whispers.

This book is born from that whisper. ***The Soul In Yourself*** is for anyone who feels tired but does not know why. For those who feel lost even when everything appears fine on the outside. It is not a guide filled with rules, and it is not here to fix you. It is a quiet companion, one that walks with you, sits beside you in your thoughts, and reminds you of the strength you already have.

Resilience, in this book, is not about being tough. It's about being real. It's about listening to yourself when the world is too loud. It's learning to bend without breaking, to cry without shame, to fall and rise again with grace.

Each chapter is part of a journey, beginning with the first spark of awareness, moving through doubt and discomfort, and gradually leading toward purpose and peace. It explores emotional strength, mental flexibility, and spiritual steadiness, not in complicated terms but through stories, reflections, and small truths that anyone can relate to in a modern-day scenario.

The structure of this book from Gentle Welcome to The Sole Reclaimed, follows the natural rhythm of growth. Just like the seasons shift, like the lotus rises from muddy waters, this path leads you from uncertainty toward clarity, not in one leap, but through gentle steps.

If you are reading this, perhaps some part of you is ready. Ready to reconnect with your inner voice. Ready to stop pretending and begin healing. I hope this book will feel like a warm light in your hands, a small lamp that does not demand attention but helps you see.

Reason for writing this book

This book arose from a deep desire to illuminate the untold stories of quiet strength, including the moments people endure silently, the small decisions that shape character, and the inner voices that are often drowned out by doubt or distraction.

Life often tests us in quiet ways. It is not always dramatic or loud. Sometimes, it is simply a silent ache, such as a sleepless night, a heavy moment at the kitchen sink, or a feeling of being invisible even when surrounded by people. We carry so much, yet we rarely speak about what it means to truly feel strong within.

This book was written to speak to those quiet places.

Mahua Sil Sett has spent years observing how resilience is often misunderstood. It is not just about being brave in times of crisis. True resilience is about everyday courage, the kind that helps you rise when no one is watching, make kind choices when you feel drained, and believe in yourself even when doubt begins to creep in.

She recognized how quietly people endure their struggles, especially in the world we live in today. Behind smiles, in homes, in conversations that never go deep enough. That's why she wrote "**The Soul In Yourself**". To give those silent stories a voice. To remind readers that their feelings are valid, their struggles are real, and their inner strength is still intact.

Her hope is that this book becomes a mirror, a soft space where people can see their own strength not as something they have to earn, but as something they already carry. Through real stories, simple reflections, and gentle insights, she wants readers to understand that resilience does not mean avoiding pain; it means growing through it.

It's not about becoming someone new. It's about remembering who you've always been.

Unique features of this book

This book was crafted with great care, not only in what it says but also in how it feels. Every part of it was shaped to offer comfort, clarity, and quiet strength. *The Soul In Yourself* is not just about ideas; it is about experiences that touch the heart and reflections that remain with you long after the page is turned.

Here's what makes it special:

A Gentle and Natural Flow: The chapters follow a thoughtful rhythm, from *The Spark of Self* to *The Soul Reclaimed*. This structure reflects life's natural journey: moments of awakening, trials and growth, and the gentle return to inner peace. It is not rushed. It does not demand. It moves like seasons, inviting, patient, and full of meaning.

The Three Pillars of Inner Resilience

Resilience is explored through three key aspects:

> **Emotional Endurance** – Learning how to stay soft but steady through emotional ups and downs.
>
> **Mental Flexibility** – Gaining tools to think clearly and adapt when things change or feel uncertain.
>
> **Spiritual Groundedness** – Staying anchored in values, beliefs, and the quiet wisdom within.

These pillars are not presented as distant ideas. They are offered as living practices, ones you can build, grow into, and carry with you.

Real-Life Reflections

The book offers gentle guidance through simple, relatable moments from everyday life. Instead of presenting big lessons, it shares small truths, such as choosing kindness during times of stress, pausing to reflect rather than reacting, or trusting your own voice when others are loud. These reflections help readers feel seen and understood.

Blending Story with Soul

Throughout the book, you'll find stories, symbols, and metaphors that help deepen each message. From the image of a lotus blooming in muddy waters to the quiet strength of a clay lamp glowing in darkness, each example brings warmth and clarity. Cultural wisdom and nature's teachings are gently woven in, offering light from many directions.

This book is not just a guide. It is a gentle companion for anyone learning to listen to themselves, rediscover their courage, and live with quiet purpose.

About the writer

Mahua Sil Sett was born in *Chinsurah*, a riverside town steeped in Bengal's history and quiet charm. From childhood, she carried within her the serene strength of her heritage. Her inner poise was shaped not by privilege, but through perseverance, boundless curiosity, and a love for learning that never dimmed.

Mahua Sil Sett pursued her education through government institutions, starting with school and continuing through university and law college. Her academic journey was shaped by grit and grace. With a Master's degree in Economics and legal training as an advocate, she built a foundation rooted in knowledge. Yet, her greatest lessons were taught not in classrooms, but by life itself.

After marriage, she embraced the role of homemaker in Kolkata. Yet her mind remained quietly ablaze, finding meaning not just in books, but in daily moments: the silence between conversations, the questions in her children's eyes, the gentle rhythm of ordinary life. These were not distractions. They were revelations. Over time, they formed the heart of this book.

Mahua's writing is shaped by the two worlds she inhabits: the intellectual realm of academia and the intimate rhythms of domestic life. It is nourished by tradition and inquiry, enriched by motherhood and the ongoing journey of self-exploration. She brings clarity without judgment, wisdom without noise. Her strength lies not in loud declarations, but in quiet truths that speak directly to the soul.

The Soul In Yourself carries a voice that is grounded in truth, rich in compassion, and deeply attuned to the human experience. It is a tribute to her lived experience and her belief that resilience begins not in doing more, but in remembering who you truly are.

This book is not written from a podium. It does not aim to preach, correct, or instruct. It is shaped by lived moments, some heavy and some healing, and by the deep belief that every soul has its own rhythm and its own light. Through these pages, may you walk at your own pace, find comfort in your own reflections, and feel gently reminded of your inner power.

Let this be not just something you read, but something you remember when life grows quiet, or complicated, or real.

Resilience does not make you louder. It allows you to listen more deeply, love more gently, and return to yourself with a courage that speaks in silence.

Contents

Preface ... iii
Reason for writing this book ... v
Unique features of this book ... vii
About the writer ... ix

Introduction – The Spark of Self ... 1

What is inner resilience? ... 1
The Three Pillars of Inner Resilience ... 2
Emotional Endurance ... 2
Mental Flexibility ... 5
Spiritual Groundedness ... 7
Inner Resilience Is a Practice ... 8
Inner resilience means ... 9
1. Allowing failure to teach ... 9
2. Finding light in cracks, not shame ... 10
3. Realizing your worth lives in your essence ... 11
Why rediscovering the self - matters now more than ever ... 12
A gentle welcome into the path of self-reclamation ... 14
Gentle Welcome ... 14
The Path ... 15
Self-Reclamation ... 16
Altogether ... 17

Chapter 1: Awakening the inner voice ... 19

Recognizing the quiet strength that lives within ... 20
What Is Quiet Strength? ... 20
Listens before reacting ... 21
Chooses peace over drama ... 23
Keeps believing in small ways, even when hope feels fragile ... 25
How This Appears in Daily Life ... 28
The power of self-awareness through reflection and intuition ... 28

Chapter 2: Overcoming self-doubt ... 35

Reclaiming Inner Authority 35
Key Narrative Threads 35
Understanding where doubt comes from internal and external voices 36
Techniques for reframing limiting beliefs 39

Chapter 3: Building resilience 45

What resilience really looks like in daily life 46
Tools for emotional strength: routine, community & belief 48
Scientific and philosophical views on mental equilibrium 49

Chapter 4: Embracing change 53

Navigating discomfort as a stepping stone 54
Lessons from nature and history: the lotus in muddy waters? 55
Mindset shifts from resistance to flow 57

Chapter 5: Living with Purpose 59

Defining one's soul-calling or dharma 61
Purpose not as a destination, but a daily act 62
Inspiring examples of purpose-driven lives 65

Chapter 6: Holding Steady When Life Shakes You 67

Chapter 7: Conclusion – The Sole Reclaimed 85

The cyclical journey: back to the self, renewed 85
Encouragement to keep evolving 87
Maybe a poetic invocation or a guiding question for the reader... 89

The Soul In Yourself

— Unlocking Your Inner Resilience

Introduction – The Spark of Self

What is inner resilience?

Inner resilience is not merely the strength to endure but it is the quiet, regenerative energy that breathes life into the soul even in the darkest of hours. It is the ability to face hardship with grace, adapt with intelligence, and glow with purpose. Where outer resilience may flex muscles, inner resilience listens to the silence within and learns to sing through it.

It is shaped not only by life's turbulence but also by the choices we make in response, by the way we absorb the lessons etched into us through pain, failure, and uncertainty. Like a seed buried deep in the soil, inner resilience awakens not with fanfare, but with slow, deliberate emergence into light.

The Three Pillars of Inner Resilience

Emotional Endurance:

Emotional endurance is the gentle strength that keeps one anchored in authenticity, even as the storms of life try to unravel them. It is not about ignoring pain or suppressing emotion; rather, it's the ability to feel fully and deeply without letting those feelings define or drown you. To possess emotional endurance is to navigate sorrow, anxiety, and change while still preserving the core essence of your selfhood.

Think of the river Ganga during the monsoon. The waters rise, currents surge, and the landscape may seem chaotic, yet the river remains ancient, sacred, and enduring, never losing its way. It continues flowing with purpose, guided by a memory older than the storm. Emotional endurance is the quiet certainty that, no matter how fierce the emotional tide, an inner map guides you faithfully along your true path.

Emotional endurance, in its highest form, mirrors the ideal of *Sthitaprajna* as described in the *Bhagavad Gita* (Chapter 2, Verse 56): "He whose mind remains undisturbed in sorrow, who does not crave pleasures and is free from attachment, fear, and anger - such a sage is of steady wisdom."

This is a serenity different from Western stoicism. It emerges not from pushing emotions away, but from quietly understanding them. Emotional endurance here becomes a spiritual practice, the effort to remain fully present through grief and joy alike, without being consumed by either.

Take the Ganga once again. During the monsoon, she gathers fierce momentum, roaring across plains and valleys, rising with intensity, yet never abandoning her ancient course. This mirrors the teachings found in the *Yoga Sutras* of *Patanjali,* which speak of Vairagya, the graceful detachment from the fluctuations of emotion. "*Drishtanushravika vishaya vitrishnasya vashikarasamjna vairagyam*", means that the mastery of detachment arises in one who is free from cravings for seen or heard experiences.

Detachment, in this context, does not mean disengagement. It means the ability to observe emotion, honour its message, and yet remain anchored in your deeper truth.

In the *Ramayana,* when Rama is exiled and Sita is abducted, we witness profound emotional endurance. It does not arise from the absence of sorrow but from the deliberate choice not to let sorrow define the path. Rama weeps, reflects, and then acts, guided by the clarity of dharma rather than the desperation of grief. His endurance is poetic, philosophical, and principled.

Similarly, the poet Kalidasa in *Shakuntala* presents emotional endurance through longing. Love, though separated by fate, does not dissolve; instead, it deepens and affirms the idea that true feeling can survive time, distance, and memory without losing its purity. So, when we speak of emotional endurance, it is not merely psychological resilience. It is an ancient discipline imbued with sacred intent and quiet strength. The mind and soul speak to each other. A river flows with old memories. A yogi sits quietly in peace. A lover waits through changing seasons. A hero walks into sadness with calm and strength. The soul is like a lamp, and inner resilience is the silent, steadfast, and necessary oil that keeps it burning. Though winds may try to blow it out, the flame endures when the reservoir runs deep.

Mental Flexibility

Mental flexibility is the sacred art of transformation. It is the ability to stay open, adaptive, and creative when familiar structures fall away and the world calls for new ways of being. It invites you not merely to endure change, but to engage with it as a dance partner rather than a threat. Where rigidity fractures under pressure, flexibility bends, sways, and survives.

In the Indian philosophical tradition, such fluidity of thought is revered. Consider the ancient cosmologies found in the Upanishads, which speak of the self (*Atman*) as ever-evolving and unknowable through fixed categories. One must approach truth with humility and readiness to unlearn. As the Isha Upanishad suggests, "To the one who sees all things as the Self, and the Self in all things, there is no delusion."

Mental flexibility reflects a kind of awakened intelligence i.e., '*buddhi*' which refuses the safety of past assumptions and instead chooses curiosity. It is like Aryabhata, whose bold assertions in the *Aryabhatiya* questioned long-standing views of celestial motion and reckoning of time. His intellect did not cling to inherited wisdom but it reimagined it, fearlessly.

We find echoes of this principle in the *Nyaya Sutras*, which advocate rigorous debate and refined logic, reminding us that truth is born not from static belief, but from dynamic reasoning. Flexibility, then, is not softness of conviction rather it is strength expressed as openness.

And in storytelling, this mental pliancy comes to life. Take the character of Krishna in the *Mahabharata*, who adapts strategies and counsel based not on dogma, but on context and insight. He embodies *Yogic pragmatism*, means the wisdom to act in alignment with unfolding realities, not rigid scripts.

Mental flexibility is not just a psychological skill. It is an ancient virtue, a philosophical posture, and a graceful expression of thought. It empowers the thinker, the seeker, the artist, and the scientist to rethink what was thought, reframe what was seen, and reinvent what must be born.

In this fluid dance between memory and imagination, mental flexibility becomes the river that does not mourn the changing banks but celebrates the journey.

Spiritual Groundedness

Spiritual groundedness is the quiet sovereignty of the soul, a deep-rooted conviction that the storms we face are not interruptions but integral to the unfolding of our journey. It does not deny hardship; instead, it embraces it as a sculptor shaping the contours of our inner being.

In the *Bhagavad Gita,* this ideal finds its voice in the concept of *Sthitaprajna,* the person of unwavering wisdom. When Krishna speaks of such a one, he describes a mind that remains serene through pleasure and pain, gain and loss, praise and blame. This stillness is not passivity; it is the luminous strength of a consciousness anchored in truth. *"Prajahati yadaa kaamaan sarvaan paartha manogataan... Sthitaprajnas tadaa uchyate."* This means, when one casts off all desires arising from the mind, and remains satisfied in the Self alone, that person is called 'steadfast in wisdom.'

This spiritual steadiness blooms like the lotus, India's perennial symbol of transcendence. Though born in muddy waters, the lotus rises above, untouched by the mire that surrounds it. In the Padma Purana, the lotus is not just a flower but a metaphor for divine wisdom emerging from worldly trials.

Similarly, in *Yoga Vasishtha,* we find the sage Vasishtha advising Prince Rama that true liberation lies not in escaping the world, but in realizing the world is a reflection of the Self. Spiritual groundedness, then, is about standing in the world, not above it, but with a clarity that neither clings nor recoils.

Even in the sacred rhythms of *Bharatanatyam,* the dancer expresses this inner stillness amidst movement. It is a balance between dynamism and repose, revealing the spiritual groundedness of Shiva as Nataraja, whose dance creates and destroys, yet remains eternally balanced.

So, spiritual groundedness is a kind of divine maturity. It is not the refusal to feel, but the refusal to be scattered. It is standing firm when winds howl, trusting that each gust carries its own revelation.

It is the quiet, luminous, untouchable lotus, holding heaven in its petals though rooted in the dust of the earth.

Inner Resilience is a Practice

Resilience is not a personality trait reserved for the strong. It is a practice, cultivated over time through choices, reflection, and courage. It's built in moments when you feel least capable, but still choose to take the next step. It may begin as a whisper, a quiet 'maybe I can,' but grows into a steady echo of 'I will.'

Inner resilience meaning:

Inner resilience is not a fixed trait but a living presence within us, like the embers of a fire that continue to glow beneath ashes, waiting for the breath of courage to spark flame again. It is not the absence of hardship, but the ability to remain whole in the face of it. Let's unfold its layers through three key ideas.

1. **Allowing failure to teach,**
   Failure, is not shameful rather it is instructive. Let us understand from the story of King Robert Bruce of Scotland who had fought multiple battles to free his kingdom from English rule. King Robert Bruce's repeated defeats in battle left him demoralized, until a quiet moment in a cave changed everything. Watching a spider try and fail six times to climb its web, only to succeed on the seventh attempt, he saw that perseverance could outlast failure. The spider's determination rekindled Bruce's resolve, inspiring him to rise and reclaim his kingdom. This story shows that failure is not the end. It is instruction in

disguise, urging us to persist. True strength lies in learning from setbacks, not being defined by them.

Resilience means viewing failure as *Prayaschitta,* a sacred opportunity for reflection and renewal. Instead of internalizing defeat, the resilient soul listens to its lesson. Like a potter reshaping clay after a crack appears, resilience allows us to reshape ourselves through experience.

Example: A young student who fails a competitive exam and feels crushed by the setback may withdraw in shame. But one who is resilient might reflect on what went wrong, seek feedback, and discover a more suitable path, perhaps realizing their strength lies in creativity, not rote memorization. Thus, failure redirects, not reduces.

2. Finding light in cracks, not shame

This idea echoes kintsugi in Japanese philosophy is the art of repairing broken pottery with gold, making it more beautiful for having been broken. In India, we see a similar spirit in Bhakti poetry, which celebrates devotion born from pain. The mystic Meera Bai, cast out by her royal family, sang to

Krishna with aching vulnerability. Her suffering didn't weaken her rather it made her song eternal.

Finding light in cracks means embracing imperfection as a gateway to authenticity. When we stop hiding our flaws, we create space for connection and healing. The Ramcharitmanas often depicts the broken-hearted as the ones most open to divine grace.

Example: A parent overwhelmed by grief after losing a loved one might feel shattered. Yet in sharing their story with others, they discover shared humanity and through those emotional fissures, compassion begins to shine like light through temple latticework.

3. **Realizing your worth lives in your essence**

   Atman, the inner self is eternal, untouched by circumstance. This central teaching of the Vedanta reminds us that our value isn't based on achievements, appearance, or validation. The *Brihadaranyaka Upanishad* declares: "You are that - beyond name and form, untouched by the world."

To be resilient is to anchor yourself in that essence. No storm can uproot you if your roots grow into something deeper than transient outcomes.

Example: A dancer who loses her mobility due to injury might feel stripped of identity. But as she begins to teach, mentor, and choreograph, she realizes her artistry was never confined to her body but it lived in her spirit. Her worth wasn't gone, it merely changed the form.

So inner resilience is not a mere armor, it is light. It doesn't make you immune to pain, but it gives you the wisdom to grow through it. It is the whisper of Meera's song, the steadiness of Robert Bruce's realisation, the gold of your own repaired story.

Why rediscovering the self - matters more than ever.

In this age of endless noise, notifications, expectations, comparisons - *rediscovering the self* is no longer a luxury rather it is a necessity for awaking our self-resilience.

We live in a time where identity often feels outsourced. Social media defines beauty, algorithms predict desire, and the pace of life rushes us past our own reflections.

Many of us wear roles like masks of child, employee, parent, creator - without stopping to ask: *Who am I beneath all this?* Rediscovering the self is like returning to your own sacred center, a homecoming to the truth the world tried to blur, retreat to the mother's lap at the end of the day.

In ancient Indian philosophy, the concept of *Swabhava* one's true nature was considered the source of authentic strength. When Arjuna stands paralyzed in battle in the *Bhagavad Gita,* Krishna doesn't tell him to be fearless. He tells him to remember who he truly is. His courage is not gifted; it is revealed through remembrance.

Now more than ever, the pace and pressures of life leave little room for stillness. Young minds are bombarded with expectations and older hearts are burdened with regrets. Rediscovering the self is a form of healing that defies age and helps us to maintain the balance between expectation and eligibility. It allows you to reclaim lost dreams, restore inner dialogue, and reset your compass not toward success but toward *meaning*.

Imagine a forest path long overgrown. Beneath layers of dust and distraction lies a trail made just for you, gently winding through memories, values, and intuitions. To walk that path again is to rediscover your resilience, not through what others see, but what you finally remember to feel.

To rediscover the self is to trade the mirror for the window and to stop gazing at reflections but start seeing the sky.

A gentle welcome into the path of self-reclamation.

"A gentle welcome into the path of self-reclamation" evokes the image of a doorway not flung open with urgency, but softly beckoning, like the hush before dawn, or the first breeze after summer rain. Let's break it down vividly:

Gentle Welcome: It is the kind of embrace that doesn't ask for credentials, explanations, or urgency. A gentle welcome offers warmth, safety, and kindness. It isn't a command nor a challenge; it is an invitation offered with gentle words and unwavering patience.

Like a friend who reaches out with an open palm, not a pointed finger, it says, *"Come as you are."* For those weary from life's relentless demands, it offers rest, not resistance.

Its tone is nurturing and patient, attuned to the fragile rhythms of healing. It doesn't push forward rather it quietly walks beside.

Imagine the soft glow of a lamp in a darkened room. It doesn't overwhelm; it guides. In its presence, you begin not with effort, but with ease. Not with conquest, but with comfort. And in that space, the journey back to self begins.

The Path: The path is not paved with trophies or marked with milestones others recognize. It is a quiet, personal unfolding just like a journey that curves and meanders like a river tracing its own rhythm. It does not demand speed or precision; instead, it welcomes slowness, attentiveness, and the honesty of wandering.

This is not a highway of achievement, nor a sprint toward some distant perfection. The path invites you to walk, not run, so you can feel your feet press against old ground, where memories lie like fallen leaves waiting to be picked up again.

It leads inward as much as forward, through beliefs once unquestioned, through dreams long buried beneath responsibility and routine. It honours the essential truths of becoming that progress is not always linear, and detours often reveal what destinations cannot.

Here, rest is not failure but wisdom. Pauses become points of reflection, and obstacles unfold as quiet teachers. The path knows you are not lost but you are simply remembering your way.

Self-Reclamation: At the very core of personal renewal lies self-reclamation a quiet yet profound act of returning to one's true essence. It is not a quest for transformation, but a recovery of what was never truly lost, only buried beneath expectation, judgment, and noise.

It is the journey of reclaiming your voice, the one quietly softened over time by the weight of others' opinions. It is the revival of intuition, a silent knowing that once bowed to the tyranny of routine and reason. It is the restoration of your story, one that has been reshaped too often by roles that confined instead of defined.

Self-reclamation does not shout; it whispers. It does not urge reinvention; it invites remembrance. You are not becoming someone new, but returning to the truth of who you have always been. Like a person emerging from intoxication, slowly awakening to the reality of life.

And in this gentle stance, there is power. Not loud, but enduring. Not imposing, but radiant. The kind that says: *I know myself. I trust my path. I walk in truth.*

Altogether... To receive a gentle welcome into the path of self-reclamation is to cross the threshold of a sanctuary not built of stone or ritual, but shaped by memory, tenderness, and truth, a sanctuary born of the soul itself.

It is the beginning of healing without haste. There is no urgency, only readiness, a quiet acknowledgment that restoration begins where permission is granted.

It marks the opening of a dialogue with oneself, one woven not with criticism, but with compassion. Each thought is invited in like an old friend; each emotion is heard, not judged.

And most of all, it is a reminder that you are not lost. The path beneath your feet was always yours to walk. You are simply and profoundly on your way back, returning to the core, to clarity, to the forgotten beauty of being yourself.

This path won't be straight or fast. Sometimes you'll walk slowly, sometimes you may stop or turn around. That's okay. You're not something broken to fix but you're a story that's still unfolding.

As you turn the pages, you won't find sudden change. You'll find calm moments. You'll meet yourself again in a new, gentler way. You'll hear your own voice more clearly. You'll begin to remember who you really are. You can assess your strength encouraged by willpower.

You're not here to become someone else.

You're here to find the person you've always been.

Chapter 1: Awakening the inner voice

It starts with listening.

You are returning not to the world outside, but to the quiet space within. That place where your thoughts pause and your feelings stretch their arms after a long sleep.

Maybe you've ignored that voice for years. Maybe you thought it was too quiet, too unsure, too small. But it's still there, waiting, not for you to be perfect, just for you to pay attention.

Your inner voice isn't loud. It doesn't shout instructions or give big answers. It whispers, sometimes through a feeling, sometimes through a sudden memory, or a simple moment that feels "just right."

Learning to hear it again means slowing down. Taking small steps. Giving space to your thoughts and feelings without rushing to fix or judge them.

Somewhere deep down, you already know what you need. You already know what feels true. But the world can be noisy, and that knowing often gets buried.

This chapter is about gently digging it up again.

You don't need to do anything fancy. Simply notice. Gently breathe. Quietly ask yourself; What feels real to me? What stirs life within me?

The answers won't come all at once. But they will come.
The voice inside you was never gone.
It was just waiting for you to come home.

Recognizing the quiet strength that lives within.
What Is Quiet Strength?

Quiet strength isn't loud or showy. It doesn't need applause or attention. It's the steady, inner resilience you carry with you—the kind that endures quietly through challenges and doesn't give up. It's not about proving anything to others; it's about staying grounded in who you are, even when life feels heavy. This kind of strength moves gently, but it holds deeply.

To **endure through challenges without giving up** means holding on not with force or resistance, but with quiet determination, even when things feel hard or uncertain. It's the ability to keep moving, even slowly, even shakily, instead of stopping altogether. It's in these moments we recall the childhood story of tortoise and hare for not to give up but to try till last breath, reminding us that enduring isn't about speed, but about staying the course, one breath at a time.

Think of a banyan tree growing through concrete. The cracks weren't there to help it but it pushed through anyway not fast, not loudly, just persistently. That's what endurance looks like. It doesn't always roar. Sometimes it barely whispers, *"I'm still here."*

In everyday life, quiet strength reveals itself in subtle yet profound ways. It appears when someone continues to try, even after facing failure more than once. It shows up when a person chooses hope over despair, especially on mornings that feel heavy. It's present when you respond to your own doubts with kindness instead of criticism. And it unfolds when you choose rest, not to run away, but as a courageous act of preparing to begin again with renewed spirit.

It's a soft but steady voice inside saying, *"I may bend, but I won't break. Not yet."*

Listens before reacting.

To **listen before reacting** means creating a pause, a moment of space between what happens around you and how you respond. It's an act of inner stillness, where understanding takes priority over impulse.

Imagine someone speaking to you in anger. The natural urge might be to defend, interrupt, or push back. But quiet strength invites you to listen first. Not just to the words, but to the emotions behind them. To the silence between sentences, to your own heartbeat asking, "What's truly needed right now?"

This kind of listening is not a weakness; it is wisdom.

When you choose to listen, you allow the full picture to form before choosing your next step. You protect your energy. You make space for clarity and compassion. And often, you discover the situation isn't what it first seemed.

It is like watching a ripple spread across a pond before stepping into it. You see where the waves go, how deep the water is, and whether it is safe to wade through.

In daily life, this kind of listening reveals itself in moments of quiet awareness. It emerges when you receive criticism and choose to pause, allowing space to understand the pain behind the words. It shows up when you feel emotionally triggered but take a breath before responding, creating room for clarity instead of reaction. It's present when you notice your own anger and gently ask yourself what deeper feeling is underneath, choosing reflection over impulse.

Reacting immediately might feel powerful. But real power lies in choice and choice is born from listening.

Overcome anger is indispensable for self realisation. To transcend the illusions of ego and desire, one must first extinguish the fire of anger. Only in the stillness of a calm mind does the self reveal its eternal light.

Chooses peace over drama.

Choosing peace over drama means valuing calm, clarity, and emotional well-being more than being right, being loud or being involved in every conflict. It's the decision to step back instead of jumping in, especially when tension rises. This kind of strength isn't about staying silent or avoiding hard conversations. It's about approaching them with care, not chaos.

Imagine a moment when someone accuses you unfairly or tries to pull you into an argument. The drama invites you in emotionally charged, quick to flare. But you pause, take a deep breath and then decide not to let the moment control you. You speak gently, or maybe you choose not to speak at all. You understand that some fires die down not because they're fought but because no one fuels them further.

In real life, this kind of strength quietly emerges in your choices. It's seen when you step away from gossip, refusing to feed negativity. It speaks through the moments you respond to anger with calm, choosing peace over escalation. It shines when you let go of the urge to have the last word, trusting that silence can carry dignity. And it flows through your efforts to resolve misunderstandings with grace, without casting blame, transforming conflict into connection.

Peace is not weakness; it is wisdom spoken in a quiet voice. It creates space for healing, instead of noise for attention.

A Clay Cup on the Veranda:

Riya sat on the veranda sipping chai from a clay cup, watching the afternoon sky gather clouds. Inside the house, voices rose - her cousin Diya and aunt were arguing again, a familiar rhythm of blame and hurt that had echoed for years.

She knew the lines by heart. If she walked in, she could take sides, explain everything, set things straight. That's what she used to do - stepping into the storm, hoping to fix what never stayed fixed.

But today felt different.

She looked at her cup. The tea was warm, silent, grounding. A drop of rain landed on its rim, and she smiled, not out of joy, but from a quiet understanding. Some storms aren't meant to be entered. Some peace is worth protecting.

Instead of reacting, she stayed where she was. She listened. The voices faded. The rain grew louder. Slowly, the storm passed both outside and in.

That evening, Diya joined her silently on the veranda. No apology. No explanation. Just two cups. Two hearts choosing stillness.

That was her quiet strength. Not her silence but her choice to let calm lead.

Keeps believing in small ways, even when hope feels fragile.

To **keep believing in small ways even when hope feels fragile** is like lighting tiny lamps in the dark not because you're sure the sun is rising, but because you refuse to stop looking for it.

This kind of belief doesn't roar. It whispers. It comes through small choices: putting one foot forward when the road is unclear, leaving space in your heart for joy even on difficult days, trusting that your efforts matter even if no one sees them yet.

The passage of time may not mend everything, but it eases us into acceptance of reality and to try our best for reaching in comfort zone.

Imagine a farmer sowing seeds before the rain. The sky is dry, the season uncertain. But he plants anyway. Not with certainty, but with quiet faith. He doesn't need loud guarantees just a sense that maybe, just maybe, something will grow.

In real life, this kind of strength quietly emerges in your choices. It's seen when you step away from gossip, refusing to feed negativity. It speaks through the moments you respond to anger with calm, choosing peace over escalation. It shines when you let go of the urge to have the last word, trusting that silence can carry dignity. And it flows through your efforts to resolve misunderstandings with grace, without casting blame, turning conflict into connection.

It's the kind of hope that sits quietly in your chest and says, *"I will try again. Not* because *it's easy, but because something inside me still believes."*

It's the strength that stays when everything else feels uncertain. It doesn't need attention. It just *is*.

A Simple Illustration:

Imagine a small clay lamp, the kind lit during Diwali. It flickers in a quiet room. Outside, there's noise, storms, distractions but the flame stays steady. It's not big. It doesn't roar. Yet it lights the darkness around it, moment by moment.

Your quiet strength is like that flame.

People may not always notice it. You may forget it is burning. But it is there: warm, steady, alive. It has always been with you. And now, you are beginning to see it again.

Self-realization blooms not through hurried strides or rivalry, but through the quiet persistence of steady steps taken in peace.

How This Appears in Daily Life

Quiet strength shines through your everyday choices in the most unassuming ways. It's there when you soothe yourself after a difficult day, trusting your own comfort without seeking anyone's approval. It speaks softly but firmly when you say no with gentleness and sincerity. It unfolds when you choose rest not out of laziness, but because you recognize that peace is something you deserve. And it glows in those quiet moments when you look at your reflection and stop judging yourself, offering compassion instead.

Every time you pause, reflect, breathe, and choose with care you're living from that inner strength.

When we sleep, our body finds rest but the mind often remains active. True mental rest comes not only through sleep, but through moments of quiet reflection. When you sit in stillness and gently speak with yourself, the mind begins to settle. In that silence, it finds its own form of rest.

The power of self-awareness through reflection and intuition.

Self-awareness through reflection and intuition is like looking into a quiet pond you begin to see yourself more clearly, not through the stories others told you, but through your own presence.

Reflection is the act of gently turning inward. It's asking yourself honest questions like: *"How did that moment make me feel?"* or *"Why did I react that way?"* It doesn't rush for answers, it allows space for truth to surface. The more you reflect, the more you notice your patterns, your emotional waves, your hidden desires. You begin to see what nourishes you and what drains you.

Intuition, on the other hand, is your inner compass. It's the subtle pull, the quiet whisper that guides you before logic fully catches up. It's that strange yet familiar sense that says *"This feels right"* or *"Something's off here."* You can't always explain it but you can feel it. And with reflection, your intuition grows stronger, clearer, more reliable.

Together, reflection and intuition help you reconnect with your deeper self. They lead you to make choices based not on noise or fear, but on what truly aligns with who you are becoming. It's like tuning an instrument so that you learn your natural rhythm, your true tone, and eventually, you begin to live in harmony with it.

The Umbrella at the Bus Stop

Pihu stood under the broken awning of the bus stop, watching the grey sky stitch droplets into the street. Her umbrella sat unopened in her bag. She hadn't felt the need for it, yet everyone else had theirs up, rushing, shielding, moving fast.

She stayed still.

Her instinct told her the rain wasn't heavy enough, not yet. But a part of her wondered if she should follow the crowd just in case. That familiar tug: *"Maybe I'm wrong. Maybe I should act."*

She placed her hand out and caught the rain. It was warm, gentle, almost playful. Not a threat. A memory stirred, her grandmother saying, *"If you always react first, you'll never know what it was like to feel."*

So Pihu waited.

She watched the people with umbrellas rush by, frowns on their faces, heads ducked. And she stood there, present, listening to both the world and the quiet inside. Her body relaxed, her mind softened. She realized the rain didn't need escaping. It needed noticing.

She took a deep breath. Not from logic. Not from instruction. Just from a soft voice inside saying, *"It's okay to be here. It's okay to trust yourself."*

The bus arrived. She boarded, slightly wet but deeply calm. For the first time in a long time, she felt like she hadn't just passed through a moment but she had truly lived inside it.

That was her self-awareness. That was her intuition. Not loud. Not dramatic. Just real.

On a rain-kissed morning, with droplets still falling lightly on the leaves, a mother bird sat in her nest. Her newborns moved gently beside her, hungry and expectant. She had food saved, enough to calm their cries. Still, something in her, a quiet instinct, told her the rain would soon stop. She waited, not because she had to, but because she wanted to. She hoped to give her children not just nourishment, but something fresh from the earth. As the clouds began to clear and light broke through, she prepared to fly. Her wings, steady and patient, carried more than food. They carried her trust.

Personal anecdote or metaphor to illustrate: perhaps the story of *Nachiketa* from the *Upanishads*?

The story of *Nachiketa* from the *Kathopanishad* is a rich and timeless metaphor that beautifully illustrates self-awareness, reflection, intuition, and the quiet strength of inner seeking. Here's a simple retelling shaped to resonate within Chapter 1's gentle tone, like a whisper of wisdom woven into the journey:

The Boy Who Questioned Death

In a quiet ancient village, there lived a boy named Nachiketa. He was thoughtful, deep in ways most children weren't. One day, his father performed a great ritual, offering wealth and gifts to gain favour from the gods. But Nachiketa saw through it. He felt something wasn't right.

"Father," he asked, "Why offer what you no longer need? Isn't truth more important than appearance?"

His father, angered and ashamed, lashed out: "Go to Death!" And so, the boy did.

He went to meet Yama, the Lord of Death, not with fear, but with calm curiosity. He waited patiently for three days at Yama's door. When the deity returned, impressed by his resolve, he offered Nachiketa three boons.

For the final boon, Nachiketa asked the deepest question: "What happens after death? What is the nature of the self?"

Yama tried to dissuade him offering riches, long life, pleasures instead. But Nachiketa gently refused. "These things fade. I want to know what lasts."

That was his quiet strength.

Nachiketa wasn't loud. He didn't argue or demand. He simply listened to his inner voice, followed it into the unknown, and stood firm in the face of distraction.

And in that stillness, that self-awareness, Yama revealed the secret: the soul is eternal, untouched by death, pure consciousness - *Atman*.

Just like Nachiketa, the readers of your chapter are being invited to pause, reflect, and listen to that quiet voice inside. It is the voice that does not settle for surface answers, the one that asks, *"What is truly real for me?"*

Nachiketa's story tells us that inner wisdom isn't loud or complex. It's steady. It comes from daring to question, holding silence, and walking inward with courage.

Collecting knowledge and experience do not make you wise, but self-analysis of all these enrich your inner wisdom as well as self-reliance.

Chapter 2: Overcoming self-doubt

Reclaiming Inner Authority

Self-doubt often arises in silence. It slips in like mist soft, unannounced, yet capable of dimming the brightest light within. This chapter is about meeting that mist with warmth, not war. Not as something to destroy, but as something to understand.

We begin with the idea that doubt is not the enemy but it is the invitation, it is a chance of reviewing yourself.

Key Narrative Threads

The Nature of Self-doubt: Self-doubt is deeply a human instinct. It reflects a disconnection from one's own worth and wisdom. But it is also a teacher, revealing where healing is needed.

Modern and Ancient Mirror Blend a contemporary vignette perhaps a character hesitating to speak up in a team meeting with a tale from Indian wisdom. A beautiful parallel could be found in the story of Arjuna on the battlefield, paralyzed by self-doubt, needing Krishna to remind him of his dharma and inner strength.

The Gentle Pivot Show how self-doubt shifts when met with patience. Through journaling, solitude, dialogue with a mentor, or rituals of reconnection, one can gradually rebuild trust in the Self.

When faced with the fog of indecision, whether to act or to hold back, listen closely. The mind often whispers not what is convenient, but what aligns with your deeper sense of right.

Understanding where doubt comes from internal and external voices.

Self-doubt rarely arrives alone. It often wears the shape of other people's words or echoes in the voice you've grown used to hearing inside your head.

Sometimes it begins outside you: A parent's silence when you needed encouragement. A teacher's raised eyebrow. A friend's offhand remark. These small moments plant seeds that suggesting you're not enough, not ready, not quite right. Over time, those voices become absorbed until they sound like your own.

Then doubt begins to speak from within. It questions your choices: *"Are you sure?"* It rewrites your strengths: *"But what if it was just luck?"* It fears your expression: *"Don't say that you'll look foolish."*

This internal voice isn't your enemy. It's a voice trying to protect you. It learned to whisper caution from years of trying to fit in, avoid rejection, stay safe. But what kept you safe then might be keeping you small now.

To understand doubt is to ask gently: **Whose voice is this? Where did I first hear it? Is it still serving me?**

You begin to separate inherited fear from inner truth. You learn to hold space for that doubtful voice, but not follow it blindly. You listen but you don't let it led.

And slowly, in that quiet pause between thought and reaction, the true voice, the one that believes, affirms, and remembers and finally finds room to speak.

The Garden of Voices *A quiet metaphor for recognizing the difference between outer echoes and inner truth*

Example: Mili stood at the edge of a garden she hadn't visited in years.

It wasn't made of flowers or fountains but voices. Each plant whispered something: tall reeds that murmured, "Be careful," thorned vines that cautioned, "Don't dream too big," and low shrubs that repeated, "You're not quite ready." She had planted them unknowingly, each echoing something. Someone once said the words picked up through childhood glances, well-meaning advice, and moments of silence that stung more than sound.

For years, she thought the garden was hers. But now, something in her stirred not in defiance, but in quiet curiosity.

She walked deeper into the garden. The air trembled gently with murmurs, but beneath them was something else. A hush. A silence that wasn't empty, but listening.

And then she heard it: a voice not loud, not urgent but steady. It said only: *"You are becoming."*

Mili paused. That voice felt different. It hadn't grown from fear, it had no roots in shame. She knelt down and saw a small sapling, soft-leaved and lit by the sun. She hadn't planted it. Or maybe she had but from her own longing, not someone else's warning.

Each day after that, she returned. She didn't pull the old plants out violently. She thanked them for protecting her when she didn't know how and then, slowly, she stopped watering them.

Instead, she tended to that small sapling. The voice that spoke only when she was still enough to hear it.

And the garden began to change.

Techniques for reframing limiting beliefs.

Name the Belief Clearly. Before you can shift a belief, you need to meet it with clarity. Start by writing the belief down as simply as possible.

You might write, "I'm not creative enough." Then speak it out loud. As you hear it, ask yourself whether it sounds like fear, protection, shame, or something you have inherited from someone else. Let the tone guide you toward understanding where it comes from.

Trace Its Origins. Ask yourself gently, "Where did I first learn this?"

Was it shaped by a specific experience or a pattern that kept repeating? Could it be someone else's belief that you have been carrying without realizing it? This kind of questioning invites compassion instead of blame. It helps you understand how the belief took shape, not by judging it, but by bringing gentle awareness to its roots.

Examine the Evidence. Invite a sense of gentle skepticism.

Begin by recalling moments or experiences that challenge the belief and show it is not entirely true. Then ask yourself, "What would I say to someone I care about if they felt this way?" This helps you see how the belief is out of balance and how it overlooks your full, complex self.

Reframe the Narrative. Try turning the belief into a question or a possibility.

Instead of saying "I'm not creative enough," you might say, "My creativity is unique. How can I explore it today?" If the belief is "I always fail," you could shift it to "I've fallen, but I've also risen. What did those moments teach me?" Reframing is not about denying your experience. It is about opening up to a fuller truth, one that includes strength, growth, and new perspective.

Anchor a New Belief with Action. Beliefs grow stronger when they are supported by experience.

Choose a small and manageable action that reflects your new understanding. If you are shifting the belief "I'm not good at sharing my voice," you might write a short paragraph or speak honestly with someone you trust. Taking action gives the new belief room to breathe and take root.

Practice Self-Compassion Mantras. Create affirmations that honour who you are becoming, not just what you hope to be but what you are already growing into.

You might say, "I am allowed to grow slowly," or "My truth is not too much." Another gentle reminder could be, "Even as I stumble, I am learning." Let these words become quiet, steady repetitions that begin to replace the old voices and guide you with kindness.

Though I may not yet draw the whole tree, I've learned to shape its leaves, flowers, and fruit.

The Mirrorkeeper

There was once a quiet traveller named Shila who wandered through a forest known for its strange mirrors. Each mirror reflected not her face, but a belief she had carried: One showed her as *small,* with the words "I'm not enough." Another blurred her image completely: "I don't deserve to be seen." A third shimmered with doubt: "I always fail."

She didn't remember placing these mirrors, yet they lined her path like old companions.

One day, Shila met an elder seated by a stream, whose eyes held both time and tenderness. They handed her a small journal and said, "These are not your truths, they are reflections. You may rewrite them."

Shila sat beneath a tree and began the work: She named each belief aloud. She traced where it came from, then a childhood shadow, a voice that once mattered, a silence that taught her fear. She questioned the reflections: *"What do they forget about me?"*

Then, with a deep breath, she did something new: She chose **new words**. For every mirror, she wrote a reframe:

"I am allowed to grow slowly." "I've stumbled but I've risen." "My creativity is mine to define."

The forest began to shift. The mirrors didn't vanish, they softened. When she passed them now, they shimmered with layers. Some still held echoes of the past, but beneath them was something warmer, clearer and finally a reflection she had crafted with intention.

Each step Shila had taken; she whispered her new truths. She wasn't trying to erase the old voices only to make space for the voice that was hers.

And the forest no longer felt like a maze. It felt like a dialogue.

A story of a historical figure who faced deep self-questioning but rose above, it maybe Aryabhata's daring cosmology?

Aryabhata and the Silence Between Stars

In a quiet stone chamber of Kusumapura, a young scholar sat beneath an oil lamp whose flame flickered with doubt.

Aryabhata had spent years listening to verses, mentors, celestial rhythms and still, the cosmos whispered riddles he couldn't ignore. The stars were said to be pinned to a firm heaven, revolving endlessly around a still Earth. This was tradition, sacred and preserved.

But inside him, something stirred: What if the Earth moved? What if the stars remained still? Could the heavens be understood not by faith alone, but by patterns?

He hesitated. What unfolded before him wasn't simply science, it felt like disruption, a break from the known.

He questioned himself fiercely: Was it arrogance to believe what elders didn't? Every scroll, every chant had taught otherwise. To speak against them would not just invite correction, but it could fracture identity, reverence, belonging.

Yet one night, as the wind pressed against the stone walls and the stars pulsed like quiet truths, Aryabhata laid down the weight of needing to be affirmed. He picked up his stylus and wrote:

"The Earth rotates on its axis; this explains the apparent westward motion of the stars…"

These words were not just data. They were defiance wrapped in precision. They were the voice of one who had doubted deeply, but chose curiosity over silence.

He would go on to compose the ***Aryabhatiya***, a work of stunning clarity and abstraction, blending mathematics, astronomy, and bold cosmological claims. He offered sine tables, place-value systems, and celestial models far ahead of his time.

Aryabhata didn't prove the world overnight. He shifted it by believing that doubt could be sacred if met with rigor, humility, and a quiet courage.

Chapter 3: Building resilience

Building Resilience, opens with the idea that resilience is not a state of invincibility or the absence of hardship rather it is the quiet art of staying connected to one's essence even when life tries to unroot you. The chapter guides readers into understanding how to bend without breaking, listen deeply without losing themselves, and grow in ways that honour imperfection. It leads gently from pain to perspective, from reaction to reflection.

At its heart are themes of emotional alchemy, showing how pain can be transformed into insight when seen as initiation; inner grounding, which helps create a sanctuary within through breath, ritual, and cultural wisdom; and self-trust, understood not as a static trait but as a daily practice born through choice and presence. The chapter explores the power of compassionate boundaries, a way to guard one's energy while keeping the heart soft, and reframes rest not as avoidance, but as sacred renewal, a form of resistance to the urgency of overextension.

Pain is the flame that burns away illusion, refining the soul like gold in fire, ready to be reshaped into the form your spirit chooses.

Woven into the narrative are metaphorical and symbolic segments. One of them, *The River and the Boulder*, evokes the reader's role in life's flow: not passively drifting, nor rigidly resisting, but shaping the current with presence and stillness. The chapter also explores *Resilience Rituals* inspired by ancient Indian practices, rituals of morning silence, touch of the earth, breath and mantra as ways to root the self gently through rhythm and intention.

These ancient Indian practices draw you closer to the five elemental forces of nature: earth, water, fire, air, and space, awakening a quiet resilience within that is rooted in harmony and timeless wisdom.

Lastly, the chapter may share *A Story of Quiet Comeback,* perhaps through the solitude and surrender of Meerabai or Buddha, where resilience was not a triumphant march but a silent blooming, nurtured in sacred pause rather than dramatic action.

What resilience really looks like in daily life.

Resilience in daily life is often quiet, almost invisible. It's not dramatic. It doesn't always look like bold decisions or heroic strength. More often, it's in the small choices we make to keep moving, even when we're tired, unsure, or quietly hurting.

It looks like waking up on a difficult morning and deciding to show up anyway. It looks like pausing before reacting, breathing through discomfort, and choosing not to let anger speak for you. It's in giving yourself permission to rest when the world demands hustle. In reaching out to someone, even if your pride hesitates. In rewriting a negative thought, even if it still feels loud.

Resilience is the moment you feel overwhelmed but still choose to try again. It's when you honour your boundaries, say no with compassion, and trust that your energy deserves protection. It's in forgiving yourself for past choices, and walking forward with gentleness. It's believing there's still possibility even in uncertainty.

It isn't loud. It's steady. It doesn't always feel good it often feels like tension before release. But over time, it becomes the quiet strength that allows you to return to yourself, again and again.

Imagine waking to a morning wrapped in harsh weather. It is a day of celebration, honouring a beloved family member, and you are the host. Despite the storm, you prepare step by step, hoping the skies may clear. And even if the weather remains unforgiving, you trust that every guest will make their way, moved by love and quiet determination.

Tools for emotional strength: routine, community & belief.

Emotional strength doesn't always appear as boldness or fearlessness, it often grows through quiet, intentional habits. Three powerful tools that help nurture this strength are **routine**, **community**, and **belief**. They act as steady anchors, especially during times of internal doubt or external chaos.

Just as a seed requires sunlight, water, and oxygen, each an essential gift for its quiet awakening of our emotional strength, too, flourishes when nourished with **routine**, **community**, and **belief**.

Routine is the gentle structure we offer ourselves each day. It's the morning ritual of light and breath, the evening cup of tea, the journaling, the walks, the quiet minutes before sleep. Routine builds a rhythm the body and mind can trust even when emotions feel unpredictable. It reminds us we are held by something consistent. Over time, this predictability becomes grounding, helping us face discomfort with stability.

Community is the circle though visible or invisible where we feel seen. It could be a friend who listens without fixing, a mentor who guides quietly, a tradition we share with others, or even the presence of ancestors whose stories shape our own. Community gives emotional strength its heartbeat. It tells us: *you are not alone*. The mere knowledge that someone walks beside us even in silence, can make pain more bearable and joy more expansive.

Belief is the compass that points inward and forward. It might be spiritual faith, personal philosophy, or the simple trust that growth is still possible. Belief transforms suffering into meaning. It allows us to stand in uncertainty and still sense direction. It doesn't erase doubt but it helps us walk through it.

Together, these tools form a quiet architecture for resilience. Routine offers rhythm, community offers connection, and belief offers purpose. Emotional strength isn't something we acquire once, it's something we build daily.

Scientific and philosophical views on mental equilibrium.

Charaka's views on mental equilibrium:

Charaka, the ancient Indian physician and thinker, believed that true health comes from balancing both the body and the mind. He saw the mind not just as a part of us that thinks, but as something deeply connected to our spirit and inner nature. He described the mind through three qualities namely clarity, activity, and inertia. When clarity leads the way, the mind feels peaceful and strong. But when activity or inertia take over, emotions can become unstable, leading to things like anger, anxiety, or confusion.

Even though Charaka lived long ago, his methods were surprisingly thoughtful. He looked closely at how people behaved, listened carefully to their words, and tried to understand the patterns in their moods. He also relied on ancient teachings and wise mentors to guide his thinking. He believed that changes in the body's energy could affect the mind. For instance, when the energy is too dry and fast-moving, a person might feel anxious; when it's too fiery, anger might arise; when it's heavy and slow, sadness or dullness can appear.

But Charaka didn't stop at diagnosis rather he believed healing the mind was about much more than medicine. He encouraged people to live with purpose, to meditate, to build strong and kind relationships, and to follow simple, meaningful daily routines. To him, mental peace came from how we live, think, and connect to something deeper than ourselves. His view combines science and spirit, observation and wisdom, forming a gentle, holistic path toward emotional equilibrium.

A dusk-coloured courtyard in Varanasi, warm with the scent of jasmine.

Ishaan sat beneath the tamarind tree as twilight slid across the bricks like a soft breath. The day had been restless—thoughts jumping like sparrows, emotions tugging like scattered winds. But here, in this hour of slowing light, something shifted.

He watched the rhythm of life unfold with deliberate ease: a potter's wheel turning steadily at the far end of the alley, the call of evening prayers rising in measured cadence, a child tracing rangoli patterns for no reason other than joy.

I've lived too many days chasing the fire of urgency, Ishaan thought. But Charaka was right; peace is not born in the chase. *It rises from the quiet balance between movement and stillness.*

He brought his hand to his heart. It beat not with anxiety, but with awareness. The teachings echoed softly: *Sattva* for clarity, *Rajas* for drive, *Tamas* for rest. All must exist, but only when held in harmony.

His mind didn't feel empty; it felt spacious. Like the Ganges itself, carrying what must be carried without clinging..

Tomorrow he would rise again, light the lamp at dawn, walk slowly through the market, speak with intention. No dramatic overhaul. Just daily gentleness, as Charaka taught: in routine, in community, and in trust, in the soul's quiet compass.

Chapter 4: Embracing change

The air felt different, though nothing had visibly shifted. It wasn't the season or the sky, it was something quieter, something internal. A whisper beneath the day's ordinary rhythm. She didn't name it at first, this stirring of restlessness wrapped in calm. It was not a need to escape, but a gentle noticing. The path that once offered comfort had begun to feel narrow.

There was no dramatic break, no thunder of transformation. Just a quiet evening and the faint trace of longing for renewal, for breath, for the possibility that things could be different. She traced her finger along the spine of a book she hadn't opened in years, paused at the window, and watched the light soften against the far wall. The world looked the same. She did not.

To embrace change, she realized, wasn't about tearing away from the past. It was about giving herself permission to grow beyond it. Like a tree leaning toward light, not rejecting its roots, but trusting its reach.

Who is she? She is your inner resilience, which do not change dramatically, its changed by the process of evolution, so it is strong and sustainable.

"**Embracing Change**" can become a gentle turning point in your book, where the inner terrain begins to shift, not with force, but with quiet permission.

Imagine this moment: The character has been walking a familiar path for years, their routines shaped by safety and known patterns. But one evening, perhaps after a quiet conversation or a solitary walk through an old part of town, something soft inside begins to ask, *What if change doesn't mean loss but transformation?*

They sit by a window, the curtain brushing their shoulder, a fading sunset casting gold across old walls. Their thoughts, once tangled with fear, now begin to unfurl like monsoon leaves meeting rain for the first time. They don't rush toward a new life, they lean toward it slowly, reflectively.

Through their internal reflections, you could show how change isn't dramatic, it arrives like a new language whispered gently. The character might not know what's coming next, but they feel ready to listen. Ready to bend, not break. That's the heart of embracing change.

Navigating discomfort as a stepping stone.

Discomfort isn't just something to avoid, it can be a quiet guide toward growth. When we face situations that feel uneasy or unfamiliar, our first instinct might be to resist or retreat. But often, those uncomfortable moments are exactly where change begins. Just like walking into cold water slowly before swimming, discomfort gives the body and heart time to adjust. It challenges us, but it also teaches us what we're capable of.

"Survival of the fittest" and "Necessity is the mother of invention" are two timeless lessons that teach us how life demands both adaptability and ingenuity. In situations beyond human control, we must learn to adjust with grace. But where even the slightest human effort can spark change, we are called to persist again and again, without surrendering hope. Because resilience is not just endurance; it is the quiet resolve to keep shaping our path where possible.

Moving through discomfort means staying present with what feels hard and listening to what it's trying to show us. It can reveal hidden fears, old habits, or new desires. And with each small step forward, we build confidence and learn resilience. The more we face it, the more we understand that discomfort isn't the end of safety, it's the beginning of strength.

Lessons from nature and history: the lotus in muddy waters?

The lotus flower teaches a powerful lesson through its quiet journey. It begins its life deep in muddy water, surrounded by darkness and dirt. Yet, it doesn't stay hidden. Slowly, it rises through the water, reaching toward the light. When it finally blooms, it opens with grace and beauty, unstained by the mud it came from.

This natural process has inspired people for centuries. In ancient Indian and Buddhist traditions, the lotus became a symbol of purity, resilience, and spiritual growth. It shows that even in difficult or messy situations, something beautiful can emerge. The mud represents life's challenges pain, confusion, or struggle. But the lotus reminds us that these challenges don't define us. Instead, they can help us grow stronger and wiser.

History also reflects this idea. Many great thinkers, leaders, and artists have risen from hardship, just like the lotus. Their stories show that transformation often begins in uncomfortable places. The lotus doesn't rush it blooms when it's ready. And so do we.

Early morning by a still pond, mist curled softly over the water.

The surface was calm, touched only by the occasional ripple of a dragonfly's wing. She stood at the edge of the pond wrapped in her shawl, the air cool against her skin. Her eyes followed the slow reach of a single lotus, its petals just beginning to part, still cradled by the morning hush.

She had come here searching for clarity, though she hadn't named it that. The week had been heavy with indecision and quiet turmoil. But the lotus didn't rush. It moved with patience, rising steadily through shadow and silence. The mud below, thick and silent, hadn't held it back. It had shaped the flower's journey.

She knelt closer, watching the blossom open—a pale pink unfurling against green. And in that moment, she saw her own reflection not just in the water, but in the process. *I do not have to be untouched by the mud,* she thought. *I only have to grow through it.*

The discomfort she had tried to escape now seemed necessary, like the soil that offers depth. The pain, the uncertainty, the questions they were not stains. They were stages. She didn't feel "healed," but she felt something else: permission to keep blooming.

The lotus stayed still, its beauty quiet and whole. And as the sun slipped gently across the pond's surface, she stood up still unsure, but no longer afraid of the mud.

Mindset shifts from resistance to flow.

Sometimes our mind tries to control every detail, holding tightly to what feels familiar or safe. That's resistance, wanting things to stay the same or fearing what might come next. But life doesn't stand still. It moves, like a river. When we shift from resistance to flow, we begin to trust that even the unknown can carry us somewhere meaningful.

Flow isn't about giving up, it's about letting go. It's learning to move with life's changes instead of fighting against them. That shift in mindset allows us to respond with flexibility and curiosity. Challenges stop feeling like walls and begin to feel like paths. Mistakes become lessons. Discomfort becomes part of the journey instead of something to avoid.

This mindset change brings peace, even in chaos. It doesn't mean every moment is easy, but it means we meet each moment with openness instead of fear. And from that openness, we find our strength, not in control, but in trust.

Chapter 5: Living with Purpose

Living with purpose means allowing your daily choices to reflect something deeper something that feels true and meaningful to you. It's not just about chasing goals or staying busy. It's about waking up each day and knowing that your actions, no matter how small, are connected to what matters most in your heart.

When someone lives with purpose, their life begins to feel more focused and steady. Challenges still come, but they aren't just problems, they become part of a journey that has direction. Purpose offers clarity when things feel uncertain. It acts like an inner compass, helping us choose paths that feel right, not just convenient.

Living with purpose also means being honest about what brings you joy, what you're willing to stand for, and how you want to grow. It invites you to show up fully even not perfectly, but sincerely. And over time, even ordinary routines begin to shine with quiet meaning.

Living with purpose is like planting seeds with intention not just letting life happen, but choosing how to engage with it every day. It's the quiet decision to align your actions, thoughts, and relationships with what you truly value. This doesn't require dramatic gestures. Even small routines, when guided by purpose, begin to carry meaning. Preparing a meal, writing a letter, walking mindfully through a neighbourhood, all can become reflections of what matters to you.

Purpose also gives shape to discomfort and uncertainty. When life feels confusing, having a sense of purpose is like holding a lantern while walking through fog. You may not see everything clearly, but you have a direction. It helps you make choices not from fear, but from inner clarity.

This way of living also shifts the energy around you. People often feel it, not as pressure or intensity, but as quiet depth. Living with purpose softens the noise of comparison, because you're no longer measuring yourself against others. You're measuring your life against your own truth.

And purpose isn't fixed. It evolves. Sometimes it's loud and clear. Other times it's subtle, like an instinct or whisper that only reveals itself slowly. What matters is the willingness to listen, to reflect, and to let life become a canvas where your values leave gentle marks.

When you have a purpose, its fulfilment brings a deep sense of satisfaction, and that joy fuels the momentum to seek the next. Even if you stumble, purpose gives you the strength to try again, perhaps in a new way, with renewed hope. But in the absence of purpose, there's little drive, no sense of progress, and no quiet competition within. Without it, satisfaction remains out of reach.

Defining one's soul-calling or dharma.

Defining one's soul-calling, or dharma, is about understanding the deeper reason you are here, not just what you do, but why you do it. Dharma is a Sanskrit word that means rightful path or purpose. It's the inner truth that guides your life, the quiet voice that says, "This is what feels real to me." Your dharma isn't always loud or obvious. Sometimes it shows up as a feeling of joy when you're creating, helping, teaching, or simply being present. It's the part of you that feels most alive and aligned when you're doing something that reflects your values and gifts.

Finding your dharma is not about chasing success or following what others expect. It's about listening inward, noticing what brings you peace, what challenges you in meaningful ways, and what makes you feel connected to something larger than yourself. It may evolve over time, but at its heart, dharma is your soul's way of expressing itself in the world.

Living your dharma means choosing to walk a path that feels true, even if it's uncertain or different from what others choose. It's not always easy, but it brings a sense of fulfilment that comes from knowing you're honouring your deepest self.

Purpose not as a destination, but a daily act.

Purpose isn't something far away that you search for and hope to reach someday. It's not a finish line or a grand achievement. Instead, purpose lives quietly in the way you move through each day. It's in the small choices you make, the way you speak to others, how you show care, and the moments you stay true to what matters most to you.

When you treat purpose as a daily act, it becomes something you live, not just something you aim for. You don't have to wait until you've figured everything out. Even a simple routine done with intention can reflect deep meaning. Walking mindfully, listening patiently, creating with love, or even pausing to breathe deeply during a busy day all these can be expressions of your purpose.

The beauty of this idea is that you don't need perfect clarity to begin. You only need to notice what feels sincere, and let that guide you. Over time, the path becomes clearer not because you arrived, but because you kept showing up.

Living with a daily sense of purpose means allowing each moment to carry intention. It's not about needing every day to feel extraordinary, it's about letting even the ordinary things become meaningful when they align with your inner truth.

Imagine starting the day not with urgency, but with quiet reflection. A simple action like preparing tea, writing a few lines, or stepping outside to feel the morning air becomes part of something deeper. These small choices, when made with care and attention, begin to echo your values. The way you speak to someone, the way you listen without distraction, the way you pause before reacting all reflect a life lived consciously.

Purpose shows itself in moments of stillness too. Taking time to breathe, to observe, to be present. These aren't gaps in productivity, they're spaces where clarity grows. Each day then becomes a thread, weaving together what you care about, who you're becoming, and how you move through the world.

You don't have to "find" your purpose like it's hidden somewhere far away. You live it slowly, sincerely, through presence, choice, and attention. And as you do, life feels more connected, as if each day whispers gently, "You are walking your path."

Scene: Morning light filters through a clay-tiled kitchen in a small hillside home.

Ritu rose before the sun. She didn't hurry; there was no rush. The kettle waited patiently on the stove, the garden outside swayed gently in the morning breeze, and the sky glowed faintly with promise.

She moved through her morning like someone tending a temple, wiping the counter with care, lighting a small lamp near the window, placing three jasmine petals into her notebook. Each gesture was simple. But none were wasted. They were threads in a fabric she wove daily, stitched with quiet devotion.

Years ago, Ritu had searched hard for her "big" purpose. Something that would change everything. But now, as the tea steeped and the warmth of the cup met her palms, she understood that purpose wasn't distant or dramatic. It was right here in showing up with presence, in tending to what she loved, in greeting the day not with ambition, but with sincerity.

She opened her notebook and wrote one line: *Let today be a reflection of what I value.* Then she stepped out into the sun, barefoot on the dewy stone path. Life didn't feel like something she had to chase anymore. It felt like something she was gently shaping, one breath, one act, one moment at a time.

In their later years, elders often spend long hours in prayer not to ask for anything, but to anchor their minds in peace. Their devotion becomes a quiet sanctuary, a way to keep restless or negative thoughts at bay, and to remain close to the quiet grace they find in God's name.

Inspiring examples of purpose-driven lives.

The Weaver of Light

In a small village nestled between forest and river, lived a woman named Sita. She wasn't known beyond the valley, and she didn't seek recognition. Her days were spent weaving threads of cotton, silk, and wool into shawls, tapestries, and blankets. But her weaving was more than craft. It was her way of listening to the world.

Each morning, Sita sat by her loom and whispered a prayer, not for success, but for clarity. She believed that every thread carried intention, and that her work could hold warmth not just for the body, but for the soul. Villagers often said her shawls felt like being held by someone who truly understood you.

Years passed, and Sita's woven pieces began to travel, carried by pilgrims, gifted to grieving families, wrapped around newborns. People said they could feel something in the fabric: a quiet strength, a sense of being seen.

One day, a young traveller arrived, seeking Sita. He had heard stories of her work and wanted to learn. But Sita didn't teach technique. She taught presence. "Weaving is not about the pattern," she said. "It's about the silence between the threads. That's where purpose lives."

The traveller stayed, learned, and eventually carried the practice to distant places. Sita remained in her village, still weaving, still listening. She never sought legacy but her purpose had already become one.

Chapter 6: Holding Steady When Life Shakes You

"Sometimes, the path that glitters leads away from the garden of your soul. To walk the quieter trail, one lined with thorns of doubt and scented with truth, is to honor the voice within."

Life unfolds as a tapestry woven with desires, destinies, and difficulties. Along this winding path, we encounter moments of triumph as well as times of deep uncertainty. There are days when we are embraced by the warmth of companionship, and others when silence becomes our only witness. In those solitary hours, we are invited to awaken the quiet force within the soul in ourselves, a reservoir of resilience often hidden beneath the surface.

Some situations test more than our emotions; they challenge our ethics and our sense of clarity. These are the crossroads where decisions must be made with a calm mind and a listening heart. It is in these moments that we learn to trust the whisper of our inner strength, even when the world around us is filled with noise and doubt.

To hold steady when life shakes us is not about resisting the storm. It is about anchoring ourselves in truth, preparing for struggle, embracing discomfort, and rising above the criticism that seeks to weaken our resolve. This chapter explores those quiet trials where courage is felt rather than displayed, and offers reflections and responses to help us stand tall when the ground beneath us begins to tremble.

Let us explore how inner strength reveals itself in everyday moments, and how it can be nurtured through thoughtful, practical approaches.

The Promotion That Challenges Your Values

Scenario: You are offered a promotion that promises prestige and a significant pay raise. On the surface, it appears to be a rewarding opportunity. However, accepting the role would require you to compromise your ethics or work in an environment that feels toxic and misaligned with your values.

Inner Strength Moment: This is a moment where inner strength must guide your decision. Choosing integrity over advancement may not be easy, but it reflects a deeper commitment to your truth.

Solution: To navigate this situation, take time to reflect on your long-term goals and core values. Ask yourself, *"Will this role help me grow in the direction I truly want?"* If the answer is no, consider negotiating the terms of the offer or respectfully declining it. True success is not measured by titles or income alone, it is defined by how closely your choices align with your principles.

The Presentation That Triggers Self-Doubt

Scenario: You are preparing for an important presentation that holds the potential to influence your career or personal growth. As the moment draws near, imposter syndrome begins to creep in. Despite your thorough preparation, you feel unqualified and question whether your voice deserves to be heard.

Inner Strength Moment: Your strength is revealed in the choice to proceed in spite of fear. It is the quiet courage of standing in your truth and trusting that your presence matters, even when self-doubt tries to convince you otherwise.

Solution: Support yourself with affirmations such as "I am prepared" and "My voice matters." Take time to visualize a successful outcome, imagining yourself speaking with clarity and confidence. Focus on the effort you have invested rather than striving for perfection. Confidence grows through action, and each step forward reinforces your belief in yourself.

The Breakup That Shakes Your Identity

Scenario: A meaningful relationship comes to an end, leaving you feeling disoriented and emotionally raw. You begin to question your worth and find it difficult to imagine a path forward. The loss feels not only personal but deeply tied to your sense of identity.

Inner Strength Moment: Your strength emerges in the quiet act of rebuilding your sense of self. It is the decision to turn inward, to rediscover who you are beyond the relationship, and to trust that your wholeness was never dependent on another person.

Solution: Begin by reconnecting with activities that bring you genuine joy and a sense of purpose. Surround yourself with friends who uplift and support you. Use journaling as a gentle tool to process your emotions and reflect on your journey. Remind yourself that healing does not follow a straight path, and your value remains intact, regardless of who stays or leaves. You are enough, just as you are.

The Parenting Overwhelm

Scenario: You find yourself juggling the demands of work, home, and parenting, often feeling stretched beyond your limits. Despite your best efforts, a sense of failure begins to creep in, as if you are falling short in every role you hold.

Inner Strength Moment: Your strength is revealed in the choice to respond with compassion rather than criticism. It is the gentle reminder to yourself that love is not measured by perfection, but by presence, patience, and care.

Solution: Take a moment to pause and breathe. Acknowledge that parenting is one of the most challenging and emotionally complex journeys, and that no one does it flawlessly. Allow yourself to ask for help when you need it, and recognize the value in small victories. Whether it is a shared laugh, a quiet hug, or a moment of calm, these are the signs that your love and effort are making a difference. You are doing more than enough.

The Criticism That Feels Personal

Scenario: A colleague criticizes your work in a public setting, catching you off guard. The words sting, and you feel a wave of embarrassment and defensiveness rising within you. The moment feels personal, even if it may not have been intended that way.

Inner Strength Moment: Your strength is revealed in the choice to respond with grace. It is the ability to stay grounded, to listen with discernment, and to uphold your dignity even when your emotions are stirred.

Solution: Begin by separating the message from the delivery. Ask yourself whether the feedback contains something constructive that can help you grow. If it does, take it as an opportunity to improve. If it does not, allow yourself to release it without internalizing the negativity. Respond calmly and assertively, choosing words that reflect your professionalism and self-respect. In moments like these, your reaction speaks louder than the criticism itself.

The Task You Keep Avoiding

Scenario: An important task has been lingering on your to-do list, quietly growing more intimidating with each passing day. Despite knowing its significance, you find yourself procrastinating, caught in a cycle of hesitation and self-pressure.

Inner Strength Moment: Your strength is revealed in the decision to take the first step. It is the quiet resolve to move forward, not through grand gestures, but through simple action that begins to loosen the grip of inertia.

Solution: Start by breaking the task into small, manageable parts. Choose one piece to focus on and set a timer for ten minutes. Give yourself permission to begin without the expectation of finishing everything at once. Progress builds momentum, and each step forward, no matter how small, is a meaningful achievement. The task becomes less overwhelming when you approach it with steady and gentle persistence.

The Career That No Longer Fits

Scenario: You find yourself in a job that no longer brings fulfillment or a sense of purpose. Although the discomfort is clear, the fear of change and uncertainty keeps you rooted in place. The idea of starting over feels overwhelming.

Inner Strength Moment: Your strength is revealed in the willingness to explore new possibilities. It is the quiet courage to listen to your inner voice and honour the desire for growth, even when the path ahead is unclear.

Solution: Begin by reflecting on what truly energizes and inspires you. Consider taking online courses to expand your skills, attending networking events to connect with others, or speaking with mentors who can offer guidance. Starting a side project can also be a gentle way to rediscover your passions. Change does not have to be sudden or dramatic. It can begin with a spark of curiosity and a single step toward something more aligned with who you are becoming.

The Social Anxiety That Limits You

Scenario: You often find yourself avoiding social events because they trigger anxiety and discomfort. While part of you longs for connection, the fear of awkwardness or judgment keeps you isolated. You feel unsure of how to break the cycle.

Inner Strength Moment: Your strength is revealed in the decision to challenge your comfort zone. It is the quiet bravery of reaching beyond fear to seek connection, even in small and intentional ways.

Solution: Begin with manageable steps, such as attending a short gathering or meeting one trusted friend. Use breathing techniques to calm your nervous system and practice positive self-talk to shift your mindset. Remind yourself that meaningful connection does not require extroversion. With time and gentle exposure, your confidence will grow. Each effort to engage is a step toward greater ease and belonging.

The Financial Stress That Feels Overwhelming

Scenario: Bills are piling up, and the weight of financial pressure begins to feel unbearable. You feel helpless and uncertain about how to move forward, as if the situation is slipping beyond your control.

Inner Strength Moment: Your strength is revealed in the decision to take control. It is the quiet determination to face the challenge with clarity and courage, even when the path feels steep.

Solution: Start by creating a realistic budget that reflects your current situation. Prioritize essential needs and identify areas where you can reduce spending. Seek financial advice from trusted sources or explore free resources that offer guidance. Focus on what is within your control, and take small steps such as tracking your expenses. These actions, though simple, can restore a sense of empowerment and help you navigate the stress with greater confidence and resilience.

The Failure That Feels Final

Scenario: A project you invested deeply in did not succeed. Despite your effort and passion, the outcome fell short of your hopes. You feel defeated, as if this failure defines your ability to move forward.

Inner Strength Moment: Your strength is revealed in the choice to learn and grow. It is the quiet resilience that allows you to face disappointment with honesty and transform it into wisdom.

Solution: Take time to reflect on what went wrong and what the experience taught you. Reach out to others who have faced failure and found their way back, drawing strength from their stories. Reframe failure as feedback rather than a final verdict. With new insight and renewed courage, allow yourself to try again. Each attempt is a step toward growth, and your willingness to rise is a testament to your inner strength.

The Unexpected Health Diagnosis

Scenario: You or someone you love receives a serious health diagnosis. The news feels heavy, and fear and uncertainty begin to take hold. The future seems unfamiliar, and the ground beneath you feels shaken.

Inner Strength Moment: Your strength is revealed in the choice to embrace hope and take meaningful action. It is the quiet resolve to face the unknown with courage, even when the path ahead is unclear.

Solution: Begin by educating yourself about the condition so you can make informed decisions. Build a support system of trusted friends, family, and professionals who can walk beside you. Focus on what is within your control, such as nourishing your body, getting adequate rest, and cultivating a mindset rooted in resilience. Inner strength is not about having all the answers. It is about showing up for yourself and your loved ones with compassion and determination, one moment at a time.

The Job Interview That Intimidates You

Scenario: You are preparing for an interview for a role you genuinely desire. Yet, as the day approaches, feelings of self-doubt begin to surface. You worry that you may be underqualified and question whether you truly belong in the room.

Inner Strength Moment: Your strength is revealed in the decision to trust your preparation and your worth. It is the quiet confidence that comes from knowing you have something valuable to offer, even if your path has not been perfect.

Solution: Start by researching the company and understanding its values and goals. Rehearse your story, highlighting your achievements and the experiences that have shaped you. Remind yourself that confidence is built through preparation and belief in your own journey. Even if the outcome is uncertain, the process itself offers growth, experience, and greater clarity about your direction. You are more capable than you think.

The Grief That Feels Endless

Scenario: You have lost someone close to your heart, and the pain feels overwhelming. Each day is marked by absence, and the weight of sorrow seems to stretch endlessly. You wonder how healing could ever be possible.

Inner Strength Moment: Your strength is revealed in the willingness to feel and to heal. It is the quiet acceptance that grief is not something to conquer, but something to carry with tenderness and care.

Solution: Allow yourself to move through the process without rushing. Speak with a therapist or join a support group where your emotions can be held and understood. Create personal rituals to honour your loved one, whether through writing, prayer, or acts of remembrance. Inner strength is not found in "moving on," but in learning to live with loss while still seeking meaning, connection, and moments of peace.

The Conflict with a Friend

Scenario: A misunderstanding has created tension in a close friendship. What once felt easy and comforting now feels strained. You are unsure whether to speak up or step away, and the emotional weight of the conflict begins to grow.

Inner Strength Moment: Your strength is revealed in the choice to respond with empathy and a willingness to communicate. It is the quiet courage to seek understanding rather than distance, and to value connection instead of pride.

Solution: Begin by reaching out with openness and sincerity. Listen to your friend without defensiveness, allowing space for their perspective. Share your own feelings honestly and calmly. Inner strength is not about avoiding discomfort. It is about showing up with the intention to repair, rebuild, and honour the bond you share.

The Burnout from Overcommitting

Scenario: You have taken on too many responsibilities, saying yes when you should have paused. Now the weight of those commitments leaves you feeling drained, overwhelmed, and quietly resentful.

Inner Strength Moment: True strength lies in recognizing your limits and honoring them. It is the decision to protect your well-being, not out of selfishness, but out of self-respect.

Solution: Take a clear look at your current obligations. Release what no longer serves you. Say no where it is necessary and kind. Schedule rest with the same seriousness you give to your tasks. Inner strength is not measured by how much you endure. It is also found in the wisdom to pause, replenish, and choose what truly matters.

The Fear of Public Speaking

Scenario: You have been invited to speak at an event, but the thought of standing before an audience fills you with anxiety. Your mind races, your body tenses, and the impulse to decline feels stronger than the desire to try.

Inner Strength Moment: Courage is not the absence of fear. It is the choice to move forward despite it. By facing discomfort with intention, you begin to reclaim your voice.

Solution: Start by practicing in a safe space, such as in front of a mirror or with a trusted friend. Shift your focus from performance to purpose. What matters most is the message you wish to share. Use grounding techniques like deep breathing to steady yourself. With each attempt, your confidence builds. Inner strength grows through action, not perfection.

The Move to a New City

Scenario: You have relocated for work or family, and the unfamiliar surroundings leave you feeling disconnected. The streets, the faces, even the rhythm of daily life feel distant. Loneliness begins to settle in.

Inner Strength Moment: Strength reveals itself in your willingness to create connection, even when everything feels new. It is the quiet determination to turn unfamiliar spaces into places of belonging.

Solution: Begin by exploring your local community. Attend events, visit nearby cafés, and introduce yourself to neighbours. These small gestures open doors. Maintain routines that bring comfort and stability. Inner strength is not just about enduring change. It is about adapting with grace and building a sense of home wherever you are.

The Decision to Leave a Relationship

Scenario: You find yourself in a relationship that no longer feels nurturing or healthy. The connection has faded, and staying begins to feel like a compromise of your well-being. Yet the thought of leaving brings fear and uncertainty.

Inner Strength Moment: Strength is found in choosing self-respect over familiar comfort. It is the quiet resolve to honor your needs, even when the path forward feels unclear.

Solution: Reach out to trusted friends or professionals who can offer guidance and support. Begin to make a thoughtful plan for transition, one step at a time. Remind yourself that peace and emotional safety are worth the discomfort of change. Inner strength is not about avoiding fear. It is about walking through it with clarity and self-compassion.

The Creative Project That Feels Vulnerable

Scenario: You have poured your heart into a piece of writing, art, or an idea. Now you want to share it, but the fear of judgment holds you back. The thought of being misunderstood or dismissed makes you hesitate.

Inner Strength Moment: True strength is found in expressing yourself even when it feels risky. It is the quiet courage to let your inner world be seen and heard.

Solution: Begin by sharing your work with a trusted circle—those who value your voice and intentions. Focus on the joy and meaning behind the act of creation, rather than the response it may receive. Inner strength is not about being fearless. It is about showing up with honesty and heart, even when you feel exposed.

The Creative Project That Feels Vulnerable

Scenario: You have poured your heart into a piece of writing, art, or an idea. Now you want to share it, but the fear of judgment holds you back. The thought of being misunderstood or dismissed makes you hesitate.

Inner Strength Moment: True strength is found in expressing yourself even when it feels risky. It is the quiet courage to let your inner world be seen and heard.

Solution: Begin by sharing your work with a trusted circle, those who value your voice and intentions. Focus on the joy and meaning behind the act of creation, rather than the response it may receive. Inner strength is not about being fearless. It is about showing up with honesty and heart, even when you feel exposed.

Life does not always announce its upheavals. Sometimes it is a sudden move, a strained relationship, or the quiet exhaustion of doing too much. At other times, it is the vulnerability of sharing something personal or the silent ache of watching someone else struggle. These moments may not be dramatic, but they test our balance. They ask us to respond with clarity rather than collapse.

Holding steady is not about being unshaken. It is about choosing how to stand when the ground beneath you shifts. Whether you are setting boundaries, reaching out, or simply breathing through discomfort, your strength lies in the intention to stay present and true. Each act, however small, is a step toward resilience. And in those steps, you begin to see that inner strength is not a distant ideal. It is something you live, one choice at a time.

Chapter 7: Conclusion: The Sole Reclaimed

There comes a moment, quiet and unassuming, when the journey inward begins to hum with recognition. The terrain has shifted. The echoes of doubt no longer define the landscape. The soul, once scattered, now feels gently gathered.

This chapter does not announce victory. Instead, it offers stillness. A space to pause and witness the quiet reclamation of self that has unfolded step by step through resilience, reflection, purpose, and surrender.

The soul reclaimed is not a perfect soul. It still bears questions, scars, and dreams undone. But now it walks with clarity. It knows which voices to listen to, which paths feel true, and how to greet change not as threat, but as invitation.

Throughout this book, the reader has leaned into discomfort, explored ancient wisdom, met quiet metaphors and practiced gentle shifts. Now, in this closing movement, they return not to the beginning but to the core.

The journey ends where belonging begins: within.

The cyclical journey: back to the self, renewed.

The cyclical journey is like a spiral path that always leads us back to ourselves but each time, we're changed. It's not just a return, it's a renewal. We go through experiences that challenge us, stretch us, and at times break us open. But when we come back to our inner truth, we're deeper, softer, wiser. It's as if every detour, every fall, every awakening was preparing us to meet ourselves again with more clarity, compassion, and strength than before.

Coming back to the self is never going in circles aimlessly. It's returning with new eyes, with the courage to embrace who we've become. In such quiet arrival, there's something sacred because the self we reclaim isn't the same one, we left behind. It's evolved, and it holds everything we've learned along the way.

Renewal is the quiet miracle that happens not just when something begins again but when it begins differently. It's rooted in change, but it carries the wisdom of what came before. Think of it like a tree that grows new leaves each spring. The branches are the same, but the leaves arrive fresh, shaped by the seasons they've survived.

When a woman prepares to become a mother for the first time, even the most natural changes can feel overwhelming. Each shift in body and mind carries uncertainty, touched by quiet fear. But with the second child, those same changes often feel familiar, even comforting, allowing her to embrace the experience with calm and joy, no longer shadowed by hesitation.

In a personal sense, renewal is deeply emotional and spiritual. It's what happens when we've gone through loss, growth, healing, or reckoning and instead of returning unchanged, we emerge softer, clearer, more intentional. We start to show up in our lives with more integrity, not because we've added layers, but because we've peeled some away.

It's also a reclamation. Renewal asks: *What have you learned? What will you carry forward? What no longer serves you?* It's an invitation, not just to rebuild but to rebuild with purpose. Not a return to how things used to be, but a shift toward who you've become.

There's a beautiful humility in renewal. It doesn't demand perfection rather it welcomes authenticity. It's the soul's quiet whisper: *You're not who you were, and that's the gift.*

Encouragement to keep evolving.

To keep evolving means to keep growing, learning, and becoming more of who you truly are. It's a reminder that no matter where you are in life, there's always space to expand gently, honestly and purposefully. It's not about rushing or constantly changing for the sake of it. It's about staying open. Open to new ideas, open to deeper understanding, open to shedding what no longer fits and welcoming what now feels true.

Even when you feel settled, there's room to deepen. Even in comfort, there's space for refinement. Evolution is not a pressure but it's a quiet encouragement. To keep asking, *what am I learning? What do I value now? What do I want to bring forward?*

You're allowed to evolve slowly to reshape, to rise again and again in ways that align with your inner rhythm. Because each time you choose to grow, you honour the soul's quiet calling to become more whole.

You can apply the concept of evolution in your daily life by gently weaving it into how you move through each moment with awareness, honesty, and kindness toward yourself. It starts with paying attention: noticing what thoughts, habits or choices no longer reflect who you're becoming and being open to adjusting them. It doesn't have to be dramatic, even small shifts carry power.

Start your mornings with a simple question: *How can I show up today in a way that honours who I am now?* Maybe that means choosing rest when you used to push through. Or speaking up where silence once felt safer. Or bringing a little more intention into how you respond to others, how you nourish your body, how you spend your time.

Allow yourself to be a work in progress, without judgment. Keep learning from your experiences, your relationships, your quiet reflections. Journal your thoughts, revisit old beliefs and see if they still fit. Try something creative just to see what it stirs in you.

When things feel heavy or uncertain, remind yourself that you are not stuck; you are evolving. Every choice to be more authentic is part of that transformation.

What you haven't done yet, you can begin today. You may not reach the peak all at once, but even reaching halfway brings its own quiet fulfillment. Because every step forward, however modest, is a sign of growth, and the journey itself becomes a source of self-satisfaction.

Maybe a poetic invocation or a guiding question for the reader.

A poetic invocation at the end of your book can be a gentle and soulful way to invite the reader to carry its message into their own life. It's not just a goodbye, it's an opening. It gives the reader something to hold onto, something to return to, like a whisper that lingers after the last page.

Imagine a closing that says: *"May you continue to walk with the rhythm of your own becoming. May your days be softened by truth, your choices guided by the pulse of your reclaimed soul. And when you forget, may you remember, you are still evolving."*

A guiding question could be simple *and powerful:* "What quiet truth within you is ready to rise?" *It encourages reflection, gently nudges the reader inward, and honours the personal journey they're on.*

This kind of ending isn't about wrapping things up, it's about opening a doorway. The book may close, but something inside the reader begins. If you'd like, I can help weave this language directly into your conclusion.

And now, the journey rests. Not in silence, but in a deeper kind of listening.

You've walked the winding path, you've met your shadows with grace, you've found the light within your own chest and still, there is more becoming to come. The soul, once scattered in pieces, now gathers in gentleness though not polished, not perfect, but whole in its truth.

May these words live quietly in your heart.

May you rise each morning not with urgency, but with presence.

May you speak to yourself kindly.

May you create, connect, and continue not because you must, but because you're moved.

And when the world feels too loud, may you return here. To this softness. To this knowing. To the quiet promise that you are enough, and always becoming.

This is not the end. This is your beginning -

tender, brave, and beautifully yours.

www.ingramcontent.com/pod-product-compliance
Lightning Source LLC
Chambersburg PA
CBHW050022170726
48282CB00025B/501
* 9 7 8 9 3 3 4 3 8 9 0 3 6 *